FUNNY FEELINGS

by

Terry Funnell

Funny Feelings

Poems by
Terry Funnell

with
illustrations by
Peter Guest

The **Hallamshire** Press
1995

Copyright © 1995 Interleaf Productions Limited

Published by The Hallamshire Press
The Hallamshire Press is an imprint of
Interleaf Productions Limited
Exchange Works
Sidney Street
Sheffield S1 3QF
England

Typeset by Interleaf Productions Limited
Printed in Great Britain by
The Cromwell Press, Wiltshire

Illustrations by Peter Guest

British Library Cataloguing in Publication Data
Funnell, Terry
  Funny Feelings
  I. Title II. Guest, Peter
  821.914

  ISBN 1-874718-06-7

Contents

Preface

Thank you for buying *Funny Feelings*. As with my previous books, *Feelings* and *More Feelings*, I have endeavoured to put into verse some aspects of everyday life that have either amused or moved me in some way.

My humour, such as it is, derives from listening to comedians either on stage or radio. As a young lad I used to have some old 78rpm records of Robb Wilton, and this man above all others still makes me laugh. As a youth I particularly liked Al Read, a comedian who could take the everyday situation and, with a slight tweak of his imagination, could set a scene that would make us all laugh until we cried.

In this selection of poems I have once again put down in verse the things that over the past two years have struck me as noteworthy. Some of the poems are of a serious nature, others have a religious connotation, and some are just plain silly.

I do hope that you will find something in these pages that will lift your spirits for a few moments. After all, some of the things you have done have made me laugh, so maybe these verses will do the same to you.

Thank you, once again, to my long-suffering family for their help. To my son-in-law Peter Guest for his super cartoons and to my daughter Jill for hours of typing up my scribblings. Thank you also to The Hallamshire Press and all their staff for co-operation in the publication of this book.

Terry Funnell

TIDDLY

I've just had a drink with old Hargreaves,
He's a really good sort of a chap.
But he's taken the nark
Because just for a lark
I spilled half a pint down his lap.

Some say that my drinking's excessive
And I just can't say "no" anymore,
But I know when to stop
And I won't touch a drop
Once my legs go and I'm on the floor.

You see I'm more your sociable drinker,
I won't touch a dram when alone.
So when I wake at nine
I ring TIM for the time
And I'll have one with him on the phone.

Then I come down in time for the milkman,
Although sometimes I feel rather rough.
I have one pint a day,
Though in truth I may say
I can't stand the taste of the stuff.

Then the newsboy arrives with the papers,
But the headlines are usually sad.
Still, I don't get distraught,
I just reach for the port
And drink the good health of the lad.

Some people say I've got a problem,
That I spend too much time on the town.
I know what they think,
I should give up the drink
But my problem's holding it down.

"You see I'm more your sociable drinker,
I won't touch a dram when alone."

Sometimes I'm inclined to fall over,
But that doesn't bother me much.
If my legs get too heavy
Through drinking a bevvy
The landlord will lend me a crutch.

Well, of course the pubs open mid-morning,
And it's not that I'm bothered or care,
But I'll walk round to see
The one that's near me
Just to check it's not gone anywhere.

Once I'm inside the place I just stop there,
You see my pub has all my supplies.
They have spirits and wine
And if I want to dine
They've got plenty of crisps and pork pies.

The barman is very obliging,
But he's got an identical twin
And he seems to appear
When I'm on my tenth beer,
Though I've never once seen him come in.

Of course I can stop if I want to,
So I don't know why folks make a fuss.
I'm happy to say
That I once stopped all day
When I got knocked down by a bus.

They say that my hands will get shaky
If I drink too much spirit or wine,
But I'm thankful to say
I don't suffer that way,
I'm lucky I spill most of mine.

Christmas Day is a special occasion:
The Queen speaks to the nation at one.
So I toast her in wine
But I start about nine,
So I'm usually asleep when she's on.

I sometimes will drink to old comrades
Who have gone to that great hall of fame.
I had a good friend
I was with 'til the end,
But I just can't remember his name.

Well I must go, I have an appointment:
I'm due at the magistrates' court.
And I'm going to be tough
On a drunk who got rough,
Well I've no time for men of that sort.

VALENTINE'S DAY

I can't wait to get downstairs:
It's Valentine's Day,
They'll be dozens of cards just for me.
For a start, there's that blonde
Who works round at the pub
And she swears I'm a star from TV.

You see I've got what's called a charisma of sorts,
It's something I've had all my life.
If I take a young lady
Somewhere out to dine,
I will never eat peas with my knife.

And I still raise my hat
To the opposite sex,
Although some people say it looks odd.
You see, youngsters today don't know how to behave,
So they give girls a wink and a nod.

Good looks are a thing
I was born with of course,
I've got what they call "savoir faire".
One lady suggested I get my hair dyed,
But I really don't fancy dead hair.

Sometimes, if I find that I'm putting on weight,
I'll go down to the gym to get slimmer.
I've one woman chases me all the way home
And, by Jove, can she move with that zimmer!

If a young lady gets on
My bus and it's full,
And there's nobody bothers or cares,
It's me that will speak up to help her along:
I'll tell her to try the upstairs.

I've been blessed with finesse,
There's no doubt about that,
And it goes without saying, good taste.
So I just can't stop in with the missus all night,
Otherwise it will all go to waste.

I get heavy breathers who ring on the phone,
It's just the thing my sort attracts.
But the last one I had was from Doris at work
And she suffers from asthma attacks.

I was once at a dance with a lady one night,
And things didn't quite go as planned.
Her beads broke and fell down her cleavage, you see,
But undaunted I gave her a hand.

Some say I'm a bit of a cad with the girls,
But I know that they love me to chat.
One called me a bigoted moron last week:
Well, there's not many men can boast that!

Oh, the postman's arrived, I must hurry on down,
It's the happiest day of my life.
Well there's only one Valentine card on the mat
And that's been addressed to the wife!

PASSED OVER

Have you noticed some people get all the acclaim?
Any history book will recall,
Some names are so famous they get half a page
While others aren't mentioned at all.

Well, my ancestors could have been famous of course,
But we somehow missed out on success.
Other people just got there before we arrived
And left us to clear up the mess.

Take the Battle of Hastings: King Harold was there,
But we carried his spear and his hat.
It was one of my forefathers said to a guard,
"You could poke someone's eye out with that."

My great uncle was park keeper on Plymouth Hoe
When the Spanish Armada was seen.
Francis Drake never said "I must finish the game",
He said, "Eh, what a beautiful green!"

We were cooks in the galley on Lord Nelson's ship
(You'll recall he'd one arm and one eye).
"Kiss me Hardy" was not what he uttered that night,
His last words were "Who made that pie?"

It was my Uncle Festus that was there on the scene
At the battle they called Waterloo,
And he offered the General his best rubber boots
Because Wellington's feet were wet through.

Walter Raleigh's remembered for laying his cloak
When Elizabeth passed by his way.
But we never got mentioned for helping him out
When we did his dry cleaning next day.

When it comes to inventions, our family was tops,
But we always got pushed to the back.
You see Stephenson's Rocket was all very fine
But my grandfather thought up the track.

Marconi was given the credit for sound,
But our family know that isn't right.
The first wireless was made by my Great Uncle Sid
Who was bored with the telly one night.

If you think that sonnets were Shakespeare's idea,
Then you've been taken in like the rest.
It was one of my kinsmen who sang to his wife
While she ironed his doublet and vest.

And Yuri Gagarin was never the first
To go up in a rocket and soar.
It was my Uncle Dan who was fired from a gun
At Chipperfield's ten years before.

So you see how it's been from the first to the last,
We've been passed over time after time.
But we have become famous for telling tall tales
And that's why you're hearing this rhyme.

LITTLE ANGELS

I hate kids, I think they're a menace,
They're a pain from the day they arrive.
From morning 'til night there's no end to your plight,
It's a challenge that few can survive.

I think babies should come with instructions
And a full guarantee on the pack,
So the minute they cry, without blinking an eye,
You could box them and send them straight back.

And they'll ruin your Axminster carpet,
No matter what care you might give,
'Cause at one end they shout and spray jelly about,
And the other end leaks like a sieve.

You promise to cherish and keep them
When you stand around that christening font.
But after that day you just endlessly pay,
And the first words that they learn are "I want".

I think babies are just like the weather:
You don't know what you're going to get.
But there in the cot you can see what you've got
'Cause they're miserable, windy and wet.

You can wave au revoir to your love life,
Though you might think you've time if you're quick.
But as you undress in a frenzied caress,
It's then they decide to be sick.

"I think babies are just like the weather:
You don't know what you're going to get."

And they're no better when they get older,
They run about under your feet.
If they go to the loo, then whatever they do
There's most of it goes on the seat.

By the time they reach ten they want fashion:
Marks and Spencer won't do anymore.
So you take them to places to buy some new braces
Like grandfather had in the war.

18

They will buy denim trousers with holes in
'Cause they say they look trendy and sleek.
When they go out at night, if you mention they're tight,
They go into a sulk for a week.

Then they stay out till two in the morning,
And you have to make out you don't care.
If you say "Where've you been?" then you're in for a scene,
Or they'll say "I've not been anywhere."

So that's why I can't take to kiddies,
I can't get on their wavelength; I've tried.
So if people ask me how I think they should be,
I say I like them boiled or fried.

I've just got a job in a Debenham's store,
But I think I might be in the wars:
The pay is quite good and the uniform's fine,
But they want me to be Santa Claus.

THIS IS THE DAY

Bright morning beams shine out in glorious praise,
Fresh is the dewy grass that scents the air.
Nature awakens to the sound of joy
As every living thing offers a prayer.

Now in some unseen meadow sings the thrush,
While coltsfoot sweet unfolds a carpet gay.
Deep in the hawthorn sparrows swell the song,
Glory and praise to God. This is the day.

Trees breathe a melody into the wind,
Jostling for joy to know another dawn.
The choirs of nature swell the song of praise.
Another day. Another day is born.

Would that the human heart could be so bold
To cast behind all doubts of yesterday,
And grasp each new beginning for its worth.
Dear Lord, for this alone I humbly pray.

THE FAIRER SEX

Have you noticed that ladies are different from men?
Well they're not built the same for a start.
They go in and out a lot more than we do,
That's how we can tell you apart.

If two men disagree a particular point
We might have quite a heated debate,
But we don't scream and shout and throw pots about:
No, we're far more refined and sedate.

If a man wants a shirt, then he'll buy a new shirt,
It's as simple as that, there's no catch.
But you ladies have only to buy a new hat
And you want a full wardrobe to match.

If a chap meets a mate while out shopping down town,
He'll stop and then go on his way,
But you ladies are glued to the spot for an hour
And you'll gossip the morning away.

Take my wife for example (I wish someone would!),
Now, "a beautiful house" is her boast.
But why is it she'll say "I've been cooking all day"
And I'll sit down to sardines on toast?

And you ladies are always on diets of sorts,
Or going to keep fit and all that,
While we men don't mind being a bit overweight,
Cause we're cuddlier when we get fat.

"But you ladies are glued to the spot for an hour . . ."

And as for the use of the bathroom, of course,
There's one thing for certain that's true:
That you take twice as long to get ready as men
And you don't have to shave like we do.

And you're always off having your hair permed and cut.
Now you say "It's a matter of pride",
While we men only go when it really gets long
And we just have a short back and side.

And why do we have to pass compliments out
When you come back from having a set?
I've been seeing my barber for donkey's years now
And nobody's commented yet.

And I've noticed that ladies adore dressing up
So they spend all their money on clothes.
They have only to see something new on TV
And they say "Oh I'd like one of those."

As for underwear, well I'm embarrassed and shy
'Cause you ladies wear frillies and things,
While we sensible men always wear flannelette
And vests that are made out of strings.

So to sum up, I think that you ladies are fine,
But there's one puzzle I fail to see:
If me and the missus are both equal now,
How come she's more equal than me?

POST-WAR PROSPERITY

I AM among the most privileged of people, for through no great endeavour on my part I have seen an improvement in living standards that would have been unthinkable to any preceding generation.

When I was born, electricity had only just become a power for good among the working classes. My Auntie and Uncle who lived in Enderwood Road, Millhouses, were one of the first in our family to have their house lit by the push of a switch on the wall. Visitors were invited round to witness this phenomenon, and indeed were given the opportunity to "have a go" for themselves. This was the first time since the birth of man an area could be lit by something other than a naked flame, be it candle, or in more recent years, gas.

I can recall little of the War, for as a three-year-old at the start and a nine-year-old at the end, I almost took it as a natural event, not knowing anything different. It was after these six years of deprivation and self-sacrifice on our parents' part that things began slowly to transform my life and those of my family.

The first thing to be purchased was a gas oven. A green and cream gas oven. A "Fleur de Lis" green and cream gas oven. The colour alone transformed our small back room, which, for the whole of my lifetime had been various shades of brown from ceiling to floor. To give this appliance its full glory, the corner of our living room-cum-dining room-cum-kitchen was tiled up to the picture rail; these of course were white tiles as there was no other choice. Then the pot sink was removed and a modest unit in cream was installed; such luxury was to the talk of the neighbours for months to come.

I can't remember how long a time elapsed before our next great innovation arrived, but I would imagine it was at least a year or two before the installation of "the tiled hearth". The cream mottled tiled hearth. This, however, did not have the same profound effect on the neighbours as others, too, had by now jumped on this bandwagon.

Household chores had remained the same through our parents' lifetime, so imagine the ecstasy to be able to have in the home a washing machine, and one, would you believe, that didn't cost a fortune and, even more to the point, fitted into the smallest of kitchens. Well, this was our next venture into the twentieth century — a "Hoover Mark 1". A stainless steel tub about the size of a good bucket and a pair of nine-inch rubber rollers with folding handle was enough to drive any hard-pressed mother into raptures. For this small wonder replaced the large galvanised tub and posher (which had to be kept on the cellar head) and an even more gigantic wooden roller-wringer. Now we were really moving with the times!

In those heady post-war days when sweets were still on ration, but everything else was a general free-for-all, colour seemed to be the name of the game: any colour, but colour, and in plenty. One by one the items of furniture we had kept through the dark years, like old family retainers, were now being pushed out and replaced by the garish but cheerful formica and plastic artefacts that were changing our brown lives into glorious technicolour. Suddenly, heavily-grained panel doors were transformed by the simple addition of a piece of hardboard and a quick coat of gloss. Wallpaper of every hue threw light back into every corner of the room. Everyone was a DIY handyman.

Our next great leap forward into decadence was to have installed an indoor toilet and bath. To call this a bathroom would, I think, give it a grandeur it would not deserve; nevertheless, after a lifetime of going "across the yard" to the outside lavatory, this was, above all other things, luxury beyond the dreams of avarice. The area set aside for this phenomenon was at the end of the upstairs corridor. Much teaming and ladling had to be done to accommodate a toilet, a bath and a sink, but in the end it was achieved, and, with the few feet left over, a small table was installed with a double gas ring to boil a kettle, as we had now moved upstairs to live in the large room over the shop. This was much brighter, but my mother had the disadvantage of still having to go downstairs to prepare a cooked meal.

Over a period of some ten years, we, along with every other household in the land, transformed our little house into a palace fit for a queen (preferably one with sunglasses and an eye for colour).

Soon a thing called television would appear, and much of the do-it-yourself would disappear, but for those few joyous years when freedom was a glorious burst of enthusiasm, homes were transformed along with the attitudes and we were all "contemporary".

ARMAGEDDON

We are the great destroyers:
Look upon us and fear,
Breaking down all living things
Year upon endless year.

We are the message bringers,
Our many tongues are one,
Persuading all from pole to pole
"Get all" 'til all is gone.

We are the planet killers,
Tolling a final knell,
Turning creation's miracle
Into a living hell.

We are the empire builders,
Polluting sea and air:
Follow where death has walked on earth
And you will find us there.

We are the all-consuming,
Eating up the land,
Laying a concrete epitaph:
The talentless human hand.

We are the self-indulgent,
Each to his own reward.
Purchase, use, and throw away
Goods we can ill afford.

We are the last to profit,
Soon there will be no more,
Today merely heralds tomorrow,
And tomorrow is at the door.

IMPATIENT IN-PATIENT

"Could I just have a word with the Matron?
It's about all the noise in the night.
Only what with the clatter and all of the chatter
I've not slept: now that can't be right.

"And this water tastes off if you ask me,
It was in a jug just by the door,
And while I've been drinking, it's set me mind thinking:
It had flowers in it before.

"Nurse, I think Mr Soppitt is poorly,
I've just been over there for a chat.
But he wanted to sleep so I unplugged his bleep
And he's not said a word after that.

"What time do the visitors come, nurse?
Only would you look out for my Dot?
She's easy to see, she's got spots just like me
So she scratches herself quite a lot.

"I've brought my own hot water bottle
'Cause I've not come in under that BUPA.
But when you've a minute, I'd like you to fill it
Any time to suit you after supper.

"I say, nurse, could I have a bedpan?
Mr Briggs has had one before me.
Now that can't be fair, he can sit in a chair
And he didn't have prunes for his tea.

"Nurse! I've just taken my medication
From that bottle of stuff that's dark brown.
But it said I must shake it before I should take it,
So have I to jump up and down?

"Do you think I could have a new mattress?
I don't mind Dunlopillo or foam.
But this is no good, it's like sleeping on wood
And I'm used to feather at home.

"By the way, if you go for a paper,
Could you get me the Daily Express?
Only yesterday's stars said my sign is in Mars
And I could find myself in a mess.

"Did you say that I'm moving tomorrow?
Well, I hope that this red swelling eases.
What? The doctors have said that there's only one bed
And that's in infectious diseases!"

UP AT THE FRONT

My life in the Army has never been told,
It's a secret known only to few.
If it ever gets out, it might start a third war,
So I'm telling it only to you.

I joined up in the forces as Private Joe Bloggs,
But now I'm Lord Cadogan, alas.
And if I have your word that you'll not tell a soul
I'll relate how this change came to pass.

I was cleaning my rifle to go on parade
When suddenly who should appear?
But the old Sergeant Major who lovingly said
"Could I just have a word in your ear?"

He said, "Look lad, you know there's a war going on,
Well it's getting a bit out of hand,
And to tell you the truth, things aren't looking so good,
'Cause the plans aren't quite going as planned.

"In a nutshell, we seem to be losing the fight,
And they're wanting more men up the front.
Now they've asked me to go, but it's my weekend off,
So I'm changing with you, to be blunt.

"Now I'll give you my stripes and my uniform too
And I'll even throw in my tin hat,
So if anyone asks say you're Sergeant Cadogan,
There's nobody argues with that."

Well, in no time at all I was up at the front
With an army about to take flight.
But the Colonel in charge shouted down to the men,
"Cadogan has come — we're all right!"

From out of the ranks came a whole-hearted cheer
Which swelled 'til it filled all the air.
There was only one private who seemed to object,
He said "Sergeant Cadogan's more hair."

When the enemy heard a big cheer going up
They surrendered themselves and took flight,
For they thought that we must have a new secret gun
That would over-run theirs overnight.

"Now they've asked me to go, but it's my weekend off . . ."

When the news of our victory reached the top brass,
They said "Sergeant Cadogan has won.
We'll promote him to Colonel and give him a desk.
And a butler to polish his gun."

Very soon I was walking to paths of Whitehall
And giving strategic advice.
And, after the battle that I'd just been through
I found going to meetings quite nice.

One day the Prime Minister sent down a note,
He wanted me round for a chat.
He said, "Look here, Cadogan, we must end this war,
Now what can you do about that?"

Well, after some thought and a few sleepless nights,
I had an idea that took root.
I suggested our lads should dress up like the foe
Then no one would know who to shoot.

Well, the idea caught on and soon chaos prevailed,
And it snuffed out the war like a flame,
For nobody knew who the enemy was
As each side was dressed both the same.

On the day of the peace, the King said to his aid,
"We must give out a medal or two,
And as for Cadogan, we'll make him a knight,
I think it's the least we can do."

It was soon after that I was called to the Lords,
And they dressed me in ermine and mink,
So I'm not asked to do anything anymore,
After all they don't pay me to think.

If you visit the Lords you will see bold as brass
"Lord Cadogan" carved out on a chair,
And nobody's wiser except you and me
That it's Private Joe Bloggs who sits there.

WEDDED BLISS

Doug and Mary were two
Who to marriage were new
For they'd pledged their troth minutes before.
As they walked down the aisle
Mary grimaced a smile
And said "Look at the muck on this floor."

You see Mary was one
Who would clean 'til it shone
Anything that would come into sight.
She would get up at dawn
With a stretch and a yawn
And then polish from morning 'til night.

Now Doug was a chap
Who was keen on a nap
When he got home from working all day.
But it all had to stop
For as he would drop
She would get out the dustpan and tray.

She would sweep round his feet
And when that was complete,
She would plump up his cushions and glare.
If he asked "What's amiss?"
She would say with a hiss
"Have you got to sit down in that chair?"

All his pastimes he dropped,
All his pleasures he stopped,
His life was just travail and grief,
'Til working one day,
His boss came up to say,
"Knock off early and get some relief."

By the time he got home
He thought he'd be alone
So he got out his pipe for a smoke.
But there on the stair
Was his wife's underwear
And he thought it was some sort of joke.

So he shouted with glee
"Hello darling, it's me,
Would you like me to follow you up?"
Then a voice from above
Said, "Of course I would love,
I've left your milk cheques in the cup."

Now from that day to this
There has been wedded bliss,
Doug can do what he likes round the house.
He sprinkles his ash
Or throws down his trash
With never a word from his spouse.

You see no words were spoken,
No pots ever broken
That time Mary wandered astray.
So there's peace in the crescent
And everything's pleasant
But a MILK LADY calls every day.

"Now from that day to this
There has been wedded bliss,
Doug can do what he likes round the house."

COURTING

The day was set fair
With a chill in the air
And a drizzle that dampened the dust.
Though the sun did its best,
It was more of a jest,
It just hung like a giant pie crust.

It was Saturday noon
In a 1910 June,
With a wedding about to take place.
The groom was Frank Parnal,
A grinder from Darnall,
And his bride was Olivia Grace.

They had met years before
On a pleasant sea shore
When they'd gone on a trip to the coast.
It was on the firm's outing
They started their courting
By sharing their dripping and toast.

Frank was bold from the start
For he longed for her heart,
She was in his thoughts hour upon hour.
Though a factory girl,
She sent Frank in a whirl
For he thought her a beautiful flower.

"It was just a beginning
But Frank stood there grinning . . . "

As they finished their toast
Of which Frank had the most,
He said "This is a wonderful place."
Then with great self-control
He unwrapped his jam roll
And said "You take the first bite, Miss Grace."

She was taken aback
By this jam roll attack,
Which by now was a red sticky mess.
It all proved a great waste,
For Frank in his haste
Had dropped most of the jam down her dress.

Olivia rose
With jam stuck on her nose
But tried to put Frank at his ease.
She said "Never mind sir,
It is you I prefer,"
And gave his jam hand a light squeeze.

It was just a beginning
But Frank stood there grinning,
At last he had broken the ice.
So he asked her there and then
If she'd loved other men:
She said "Never a one quite as nice."

When the day trip was over
The two were in clover,
Olivia had given her heart.
They would walk out together
Whatever the weather,
In fact they were never apart.

Then one day Frank said,
"It's high time we were wed,
Be my bride, dear, and I'll be your groom.
Though I've little to offer,
At least I can proffer
A bed in my mother's front room."

Olivia said, "Yes,
This proposal I'll bless."
So arrangements were soon under way.
They first put up the banns
And then made all the plans
To make it a wonderful day.

Well the wedding went well
And strange now to tell,
The weather turned sunny and fair.
Olivia had made
A white dress of brocade
And tied ribbons and bows everywhere.

Frank was dressed like a toff,
And to finish it off
He had borrowed a suit from his friend.
Though the trousers were tight,
He could manage all right
As long as he hadn't to bend.

Friends decked out the church hall
And then placed on the wall
A beautiful sketch of the two.
And under it said
"Start with dripping and bread
Then just see what a jam roll will do."

RECAPTURE

It pleases me on winter nights
To cast my mind away
And see some long-remembered scene
Warmed by a temperate day.

To look upon the Malvern Hills
Softened by golden fields,
An undulating sea of green
Save where the white chalk yields.

Or walk a Scottish mountain side
Full fern and heather lain,
Cross-grained with brackish rivulets
Weeping away the rain.

To view again the Cornish coast:
That wild and rocky strand
Where dark and secret caves give way
To coves of silver sand.

Or see East Anglia's broadening realm
Where waters slowly glide,
Meandering through a Constable
Of English countryside.

To watch the thatcher ply his trade
While in a Cotswold town
And look on pastel-shaded walls
Leaning and tumbledown.

And on such days of pleasantness
To meet with fellow friends,
Exchanging tales of yesteryear
Until the evening ends.

And so I walk down memory lane
Travelling through space and time:
A treasured scrapbook of the years
That are forever mine.

THE COMFORT ZONE

Up steps that are worn with ages
And into the welcoming light
A hand stretches out in greeting:
"Nice to see you. Are you all right?"

Here are smiles that are warm and friendly,
Here are words that show loving care.
I sit in my place as always
(Near the back) for I like it there.

Here; away from the noise and turmoil
Of "getting" and "putting by",
Into a sanctuary designed
To calm the heart and eye.

Now fills the air with music
I've heard from my childhood days,
And I read the words of comfort:
"Love me and know my ways."

I have not the faith of many,
And rejoicing is not for me,
Yet still I'm content to be here
And trust what I cannot see.

The words and the hymns often lift me
But I readily have to concede
That I know of no Holy Spirit
That will answer or intercede.

I cannot ask God for decisions
Or press him in earnest prayer,
For I feel if I speak in the darkness
There is only the darkness there.

But I'll keep to my sacred vigil,
For I know that I'm not alone.
I am one of the many seekers
Who enter the comfort zone.

THE WRINKLY

I'm getting on now, I'm turned fifty,
Though I still feel I've plenty of zest.
But at my age, whatever the weather,
I'm happier wearing a vest.

Doctor says that my blood has got thinner,
But I think that's all pie in the sky.
If you ask me, the summers are colder
'Cause my chilblains hang on 'til July.

And my eyes aren't as sharp as they once were,
In the old days, by Jove, they were keen.
But last week I stood chatting to this red-faced bloke
And his face turned from amber to green.

I've decided to get some new glasses,
And they said in an hour I could get 'em,
So I went for a walk round to help pass the time
But couldn't see my way back to fetch 'em.

As a young man my teeth were like snowdrops,
I used toothpaste to keep them first class.
But now as I lay in my bed of a night
They smile at me back through the glass.

You just wouldn't believe what my hair was,
I had masses of curls on my head.
But I don't have to Brylcreem my locks anymore,
I just polish with Brasso instead.

I used to be fit as a fiddle,
I could run the half-mile like a shot.
But now if I run for a bus, I get pains
From places I didn't know I'd got.

I've a deaf-aid that just doesn't fit me,
It falls out everytime that I cough.
But I find it a boon when I'm in with the wife
With one click I can just switch her off.

"You just wouldn't believe what my hair was,
I had masses of curls on my head."

Girls don't seem anymore to excite me,
In the old days I'd call them sweetheart.
But now if I took a young thing to my place
I wouldn't know just where to start.

Still, I'm not feeling sad or downhearted,
On occasions I still have a fling.
And once I can get me state pension, of course,
I'll be able to live like a king.

WAITING

Still waiting for that blinding light
To steer me safely through the night.
Still waiting for the thunderbolt
To give my human heart a jolt.
Still waiting.

Still waiting for the open hand
To lead me to the promised land.
Still waiting for the Lord to say
"I am the truth, I am the way."
Still waiting.

Still waiting for a guiding star
That I may follow from afar.
Still waiting for the words profound:
"Fear not, for this is holy ground."
Still waiting.

Perhaps the Lord is waiting too,
For hesitants like me and you
To cast our earthly mortal qualms
Into his everlasting arms.
Still waiting.

SOWING SEEDS

I planted a seed
On a patch of brown earth
With little regard for the morrow.
For in matter of state
It amounted to nought
So today is forgotten, tomorrow.

Some months later returning,
I went to that spot
And gazed on the earth that was bare.
For the seed and the soil
And the Lord had combined
To work a small miracle there.

So each word that we speak
Is a seed that is sown
As we travel along on life's way.
Grains of hope and of joy,
Seeds of love and of peace
Are words that we scatter each day.

There are fields that lay fallow
And turning to dust
Out there in the valley of need.
For the Lord can do little
To harvest the hearts
Until someone has planted a seed.

THE WEDDING RECEPTION
(A Small Boy's-Eye View)

"Dad, this looks a posh place to come to,
Dad, why have I got to keep still?
Look Dad, they've got fruit on the tables,
Does that mean that somebody's ill?

"Dad, you know when you put your best suit on?
Well why did my mother go mad?
And what does she mean by 'You look out of date'?
Dad, what are flared trousers, Dad?

"Dad, why did that lady wink at you?
She's been smiling at you from the start.
Dad, why is your face going red, Dad?
Is she the one mum calls a tart?

"Dad, is Uncle Albert all right now?
Why isn't he bandaged in white?
I thought that he'd broken some bones, Dad.
Well, you said he'd be plastered tonight.

"Dad, what are all these knives and forks for?
There's so many I just can't believe.
I've got six different pieces of cutlery here,
Not counting the spoons up your sleeve.

"Dad, I can't wait to see Auntie Mavis:
Do you think that she might come tonight?
My! she must be a clever magician
If you say she gets high as a kite.

"Can I speak to that man over there, Dad?
Just to see if it's true what you said.
Will he often bend over to answer me, Dad?
'Cause he talks through the top of his head?

"Dad, you know that man on the top table?
The one that you call Uncle Frank?
Has he put on some weight since you saw him last time?
'Cause you said he was thick as a plank.

"Has the bride been away on a cruise, Dad?"

"Auntie Dorothy's come, I've just seen her,
She's the lady that you called 'a dish'.
If I go up and ask, will she show me that trick:
The one where she drinks like a fish?

51

"Dad, why is the man called the best man?
Is he better than all of the rest?
Then why has the bride chosen my Uncle Dave
Who sits round the house in his vest?

"Has the bride been away on a cruise, Dad?
Mam says that she's been two months gone.
And what does a bun in the oven mean, Dad?
Are we going to eat them later on?

"Dad, that looks like our daily milkman,
But he's not got his uniform on.
Dad, though he's dressed up in his best Sunday clothes,
Do you think that he'll still kiss me mam?

"Dad, that lady is still winking at you.
Dad, why is your face going pink?
Dad, why are taking me home, Dad?
Is it something I've said, do you think?"

IN THE BEGINNING

One day, long ago, before you and I,
God was pottering round in his shed.
He'd got nothing to do so was feeling fed up
And wishing he'd stayed home in bed.

Then all of a sudden he got an idea
Which even took him by surprise.
He thought to himself, 'I'll build me a world,
After all, I've got all the supplies.

"Why my workshop is full of all sorts of odd junk,
I've got bottles and wood and elastic.
I've some earth, wind and fire in a chemistry set
And plenty of sticky-back plastic."

Without further ado, he set into his task
Of creating an object of worth.
First he looked for a gap in the great void of space,
Placed a ball there, and called it "the earth".

Now, he made a mistake in the mixture he brewed,
For he'd not read the recipe right.
He'd got far too much water, it covered the place:
Not a piece of dry land was in sight.

The big trouble was, it was all very dark,
This earth that he'd brought into being.
Still, he wasn't too worried at this early stage,
After all, there was nothing worth seeing.

Still, he thought that the next job he'd put his mind to
Had better be fixing some lights,
For how would he see things were in the right place
If working on permanent nights.

When that first day was over, God made for his bed,
For he felt he'd exhausted his powers.
After all he'd made earth and created the light
And that's not bad in twenty-four hours.

When he rose from his sleep, it was day number two
And he looked at his work with a frown.
For all the earth surface was covered with sea,
With nowhere for folk to sit down.

So he set to at trying to make the seas move
In order to raise up the lands.
But as fast as he pushed the great oceans apart
The water would run through his hands.

It took him till tea-time to shift all the sea,
How he wished that his swimming were stronger.
Yet in no time at all, he'd made Britain and Spain
But America took a bit longer.

On the very next day he woke up with the lark,
Well, strictly that isn't quite true,
For he didn't make birds until day number five,
So he whistled and had to make do.

On day number three he created the plants
From the glorious flowers to weeds.
And he covered the earth with a carpet of green
'Til he ran out of packets of seeds.

When he'd finished that job he stood back to take stock
And he said to himself "That looks nice,
But people might picnic their whole lives away,
So to stop that I'll make snow and ice."

In the end he made four different times of the year,
He had spring, summer, winter and fall.
And while he was at it he made day and night
'Cause in them days, they'd no clocks at all.

By now he'd been working for four solid days
And was anxious to get the job done.
So on day number five he made all living things
And that really turned out to be fun.

He made elephants, dinosaurs, humpty-back whales,
Down to creatures as tiny as fleas.
He made man so that cats could have somewhere to sit
And for dogs he created the trees.

He made the man Adam and his lady Eve,
And he told them "Go multiply."
And as there was no television at all
There was little all else they could try.

Then he said to himself "Now I've finished the job,
I've made everything except sin."
So Adam and Eve said, "You leave that to us
And tomorrow you have a lay in."

When God rose that first Sunday morning
He took a last look at his plan,
And said "If I had to start over again
I'd have second thoughts about man."

THE OPTIMIST

I don't want to depress you, but aren't things a mess?
Well, I wonder what life is all for.
All this fighting and swearing and carrying on,
And that's just from the people next door.

All the water's polluted that comes through your taps,
It's been bicycled time after time.
We're lucky, we live at the top of our road,
But the houses below must get grime.

We've got global warming through burning the trees:
It's a problem we just can't ignore.
They'll soon be no wood left to make chairs and things,
And we'll all have to sit on the floor.

Then take acid rain, that's a terrible thing,
I stop indoors if that's about.
Well, last year at Scarborough it rained every day
And that's why my hair's fallen out.

Fossil fuels have all gone and we can't get the coal,
And there's not much gas left in the sea.
Mind, we're lucky, we've got all electric at home,
So really, it won't bother me.

All your food is polluted, it's not fit to eat
With all these insecticide sprays.
So we only eat stuff now that comes in a tin,
Well, you can't be too careful these days.

And what about all these mad cows that's about,
They reckon it easy could spread.
So on Sundays we cook Yorkshire pudding and sprouts
And we make do with corned beef instead.

Did you know that there's more mice than men in the world?
So I've took to wearing my garters.
And pollution is causing this greenhouse effect
Which means one day we'll all be tomatoes.

And I've not been too well, I've a pain down my side,
Doctor says that I'm starting with 'flu.
Still, you've got to keep cheerful in spite of it all,
Well, I know that's what I try to do.

"They'll soon be no wood left to make chairs and things,
And we'll all have to sit on the floor."

THE BRIDE

Only the nervous coughs
Disturb the silent holy air
As we invited guests await
The start of this affair.

Then through the open doorway
Comes the groom with hesitation,
As he looks for friendly faces
'Midst a sea of congregation.

The camera man has taken up
His place outside the porch,
As the sunlight streams across the nave
Like some gigantic torch.

The sound of tyres on gravel
Brings a limousine to view:
A black Lagonda gleaming
As the day when it was new.

Two six-year innocents alight
Dressed out in powder blue
With pink angelic faces
That are too good to be true.

A hum of oohs and aahs runs round
The happy congregation
And the bride's dress is foretold
At length with great imagination.

"And the bride's dress is foretold
At length with great imagination."

The groom in hired grey
Steps out to his allotted place,
With joy and apprehension
Clearly written on his face.

The Reverend Digby Fortesque
Has everything well planned,
And the well-scrubbed choir rise up
To the choirmaster's hand.

Anxious minutes now of waiting
For the Rolls Royce to appear,
Then stage whispers circulate to say
"The bride: the bride is here."

A handkerchief discreetly waved
Informs the organist,
Who promptly plays the bride's request:
A melody by Liszt.

Outside a band of well-wishers
Create a glad mêlée,
As the girl from gloves and handbags
Is a princess for a day.

New pews of psychedelic hats
Rise in a rainbow tide
For here she is, in white array:
The glorious radiant bride.

THE BALLROOM

She sat in the balcony quite all alone
Away from the spotlights and glare,
While the orchestra played a selection of tunes
She contented herself to be there.

Down below on the dance floor, a collage of forms
Circled round in a whirlpool of light,
And she mused on the times when she too had been there
Romancing late into the night.

How exciting those evenings had been long ago,
As each suitor beseeched of her charms.
She would flirt with them hopelessly time after time
As they waltzed round in each other's arms.

Then the tallest and handsomest man of them all
Would escort her back to the hotel,
And for a reward she would grant him a kiss
On the promise he never would tell.

But of all of the gentlemen, one held her heart
And he wooed her as none had before.
But fate had bequeathed that her choice would fall prey
To the ravages dealt out by war.

So now she looks on at the dancing below
While her heart longs for days that are past,
In the dark of the ballroom she relives the time
When the last waltz was really the last.

THE GARDENER

Gethsemane's soft morning light
Illuminated Mary's thoughts.
Was it three days since last she saw
Her master tried before courts?

Three days since he was crucified,
Just like a thief upon a cross,
And every hour since that had been
A time of mourning at his loss.

But now, the strangest thing of all:
The stone was moved, the tomb was bare.
Her searching through the catacombs
Had proved in vain. He was not there.

Then as she sat a while to rest,
She heard a voice speak out nearby:
"Dear lady, on a day as this
Why do you sit alone and cry?"

And Mary answered tearfully
"My Lord is gone, I know not where,
But you are but a gardener,
I fear you will not know, or care."

Then Jesus answered but a word,
"Mary," he said, "I am the Lord."
And in that instant she rejoiced,
For now she knew him by his word.

How often in our search for God
Have we, too, failed to recognise
The very Lord we seek to find
Because he comes in a disguise.

While we stand looking heavenward
The cheerful postman brings the mail,
The milkman clatters with the milk,
The shop assistant makes a sale.

The taxi driver takes his fare,
The next-door neighbour mows the lawn,
While we raise up our hands and say,
"He is not here. The Lord is gone."

Lord may we look at everyone
And value them for their true worth,
Not seeking God in heavenly robes
But finding him in men on earth.

TO JEAN

Fair words cannot encompass
All the love I feel for you,
Nor phrases of great eloquence
Would prove my love is true.
For such as these the knave might swear
Then vanish in the morning air.

I would not hope to win your heart
With flowers from the field,
Nor would I bring you roses fair
So that our love be sealed.
This would the jester think sincere
Then be a hundred miles from here.

So I will offer you my life,
Virtues and faults combined,
A season of adventure
And devotion unconfined.
For long as I have life to live,
To you alone, my love I give.

THE ALLOTMENT

I've just had a terrible season,
All my caulies have yellowed with time.
I should never have gone to Skegness with the wife
Just when they were reaching their prime.

Harry Crowther said he'd come and water,
But he's not quite as thorough as me,
And his eyes aren't as good as they once were,
Well, he has a white stick, do you see.

Goodness knows what he's done with my rhubarb,
But something's gone wrong, you can tell.
All he'd say when I showed him the patch of dead stalks
Was "Your celery's coming up well."

Now last year I grew marrows like footballs,
We had far more than we could get through.
The wife boiled them and fried them and baked them in pies
And we had them in sandwiches too.

You see I like to grow things for eating,
While the wife prefers flowers and blooms.
So we've compromised, I take her cabbages home
And she puts them in pots round the rooms.

And this dry weather's no good for carrots,
I took home a bunch yesterday.
When I showed them the wife, she said, "One thing's for sure,
Your radishes turned out OK."

And my peas have come up a disaster,
I pricked them all out like you do.
But they've grown up all skinny and not fattened out
So now I've renamed them "mange tout".

The birds have had most of my strawberries
And what they've left the slugs have laid waste.
And the tom cats round us seem to fancy that patch
So they have a peculiar taste.

Harry warned me that crops were a gamble
When I first got the key for my plot.
But I think it depends on the weather:
Whether next year I bother or not.

"Goodness knows what he's done with my rhubarb,
But something's gone wrong, you can tell."

I'm embarrassed by so many failures
So I hide every time someone passes.
I boarded my greenhouse up five or six times
Then I found I'd a crack in my glasses.

Course, I could always go in for flowers,
But with my luck I'd end up with clover.
So on second thoughts, I think p'raps my best bet
Is to buy slabs and pave it all over.

NEW YEAR'S EVE 1994

This night is special, let there be no doubt;
Welcome the new and see the old year out.
Let go the chains of doubt and apprehension;
Faith grows from hope, and hope from good intentions.
Last year has brought us to the here and now:
Ahead lay pastures green; take up the plough.

AUNTIE GERTIE
(or Her at Number 13)

It's been a sad do I've just been to,
Not something I'd like to repeat.
We've just buried the woman at number 13
The red-painted house down the street.

We all turned out to give her a send-off,
So I'm sure she'd be pleased if she knew.
And after the service we went to the pub
And, discreetly, we all had a few.

It's for certain we're all going to miss her,
She was far more than a neighbour to most.
She could tell you the gossip from three streets away,
Even though she was deaf as a post.

How she got all the news is uncertain,
She was never at home I'll agree.
She was bobbing about from morning 'til night
So there wasn't a lot she'd not see.

If ever a birth or a death would occur,
To be sure she'd be first one to know.
Well, she had a sixth sense about that sort of thing
And wherever it was she would go.

For a shilling she'd tell you your future
From the tea leaves you left in your cup.
She told old Mr Morton he'd murder his wife
So he went out and gave himself up.

She was always around at confinements,
She brought most of this street into life.
With a kettle of water and one or two cloths
She was better than any midwife.

She would lay out a corpse like the Co-op
And do it for half of the price,
She would bring her own pasteboard and white tablecloth
To make the departed look nice.

Oh yes, we'll all miss Auntie Gertie,
She was one of the best to be sure,
So we all clubbed together to get her some flowers
So the hearse doesn't look quite so poor.

Reverend Jones did a wonderful service,
And we had some boiled ham for the wake,
And I think that she knew that he end was nigh due
'Cause she'd already baked her own cake.

They say that heaven's just doing nothing,
Which will not suit Aunt Gert if it's true.
And what with there being no births and no deaths
She'll not have a fat lot to do.

I shall miss her not popping to see me
On the latest event of the day,
But knowing how she loved to eavesdrop
I know she'll not be far away.

NEXT

Oh Doctor, you just won't believe what I've got,
You'll have seen nothing like it before.
I'll begin at the bottom and work my way up.
Now, to start with, my big toe is sore.

Now, that seems to make my left ankle swell up,
So my shoe's like a vice round my feet.
And that starts up a pain that goes all down this side,
Then I break out in prickly heat.

Now, don't start your prescription, I'm not finished yet,
Can you see this red blotch on my skin?
Well, I think that it's starting to eat all my fat
'Cause one arm's going terribly thin.

You know last week I told you my eyesight was bad,
And you gave me a specialist's letter?
Well, this week I gave all my windows a clean
And now I can see a lot better.

So you've no need to lose any sleep about that,
Now where had I got to? I know.
I'd just got as far as my varicose veins,
Now, I'll tell you about my elbow.

It cracks when I bend it, and often quite loud,
And sometimes it locks in one place.
I was pointing to something, then turned to the wife
And slapped her one right in the face.

Did I mention I've got this 'ere crick in the neck?
And the wife's sauve is doing no good.
What it needs is a massage with your pretty nurse,
On a home visit too, if she could.

By the way, I've just read all the hours you chaps work,
And for what they pay you, it's a crime.
Especially with so many people around
Who are just wanting to take up your time.

Well, it boils down to this: could I have a sick note?
Now it's not that I'm wanting to shirk.
Only down at the labour, they've found me a job,
And tomorrow I sign on for work.

"Oh Doctor, you just won't believe what I've got . . ."

STONES ON THE ROAD
(A Country & Western Song)

As I travel down the highway
On a course that leads me home,
There are bright lights that would tempt me
To turn off and start to roam.
But way ahead I know my love
Will greet me at the door
And those lights are only stones on the road.

Chorus
  Stones in the road that would lead me astray,
  Stones in the road that I come on every day,
  But love is at my journey's end to help me bear the load
  And steer me round those stones in the road.

I used to be a gambler
At the tables every night,
And sometimes things got heavy
And I'd end up in a fight.
Now I've swapped the big casinos
For a home and loving wife,
For gambling's one more stone in the road.

Chorus

Sometime I find a waterhole
That offers everything
With good-time folk who hang around
And treat me like a king.
But what of all those paper friends
When all my money's gone?
I guess they'll be just stones in the road.

Chorus

They say that lots of money
Will bring peace and happiness
And others will respect you
By the things that you possess.
But if that's true, how come
The richest people look so glum?
Guess their money's turned to stones on the road.

Chorus

I don't know just how long
I'll travel 'til my journey's end,
But then I hope to find
A loving saviour and a friend.
Then I'll say to him "I made it, Lord,
I travelled every bend,
In spite of all these stones in the road."

Chorus

HALCYON DAYS

I can remember those nights at the flicks
When you'd queue for an hour to get in.
When ninepence would get you a seat in the gods
And an organ would play to begin.

When a "packamac" raincoat was all you possessed,
Whatever the weather might be,
And a week spent in Scarborough was had every year
When you'd sail the "Corona" to sea.

I can remember those radio days
With only two programmes to choose:
You could hear Henry Hall and his guest night on one,
Or Alvar Liddell with the news.

I can remember when Whitsuntide clothes
Were paraded in parks once a year.
You'd follow behind a big Boys' Brigade band
And the crowds on the footpaths would cheer.

I can remember the one day a week
When all of the washing was done:
There were poshers and wringers and steam everywhere
And Mondays were never much fun.

I can remember when grocery shops
Would smell of sultanas and yeast,
When sugar was wrapped up in navy blue bags
And biscuits considered a feast.

I can remember real fires in the hearth
And the coal bucket filled twice a day,
With a slice of thick bread, you could burn both your legs
And toast all your troubles away.

I can remember when trains were all steam
And you'd get sooted up on your trip,
When bobbies would walk up and down every street
And give cheeky boys a good clip.

I can remember when most doctors smoked
And their waistcoats were covered in ash,
They'd make up a bottle of mixture themselves
And charge you a few pence in cash.

I can remember when Handel's "Messiah"
Would be sung every nigh through December.
Every chapel and church would have its own choir
I was in one myself, I remember.

Now nightclubs and discos, fast money and cars
Are the "in thing" or so I've been told.
Still give me those halcyon innocent days,
But perhaps that's just me growing old.

LIVING ON MY OWN

I've not got much to shout about:
I lead a simple life.
I still go about my business,
But; Oh, I miss the wife.
I lost her seven months ago,
I'll not forget that day,
And nothing's ever been the same
No matter what folk say.
Of course, the neighbours rallied round;
They couldn't do enough,
But you can't expect them all the time
Because your life is tough.
My sister does my washing
And sometimes the odd repair,
But; Oh, I miss the little chats
That me and her would share,
Especially after tea-time
When I lock and bolt the door
And I'm left with only silence
Save my footsteps on the floor.
It's not that we were special,
Just an ordinary pair,
But life seemed to have a purpose
Simply knowing she was there.

Sometimes I wake up feeling
That it's time to start afresh
And I'm not too late at my age
To still have some happiness.
But all my good intentions
Very soon go by the board
When I come downstairs to emptiness
And not a kindly word.
They say that time's a healer,
So I guess I'll wait and hope,
I'll take each day just as it comes
And do my best to cope.
I'll put a brave face to the world
And cry when I'm alone,
For there's not much more I can do
Now I'm living on my own.

"LEST WE FORGET"
(Sunday Evening Service, 5th July 1994:
50th Anniversary of D-Day)

He prayed for the words he would say later on
That his sermon would be heaven-sent,
He prayed for the flowers and the birds and the trees,
And that money would be better spent.
He prayed for the Church as a body of Christ,
That its purpose on life be achieved,
He prayed for the members sat there in the hall
And for those who had never believed.

But, did he forget, or did he not think
Of we, who gave all long ago?
When "kill or be killed" was the value of life
And those that you slaughtered were foe.
We have lain fifty years on this foreign terrain
'Neath these manicured lawns, now serene,
We are silenced to tell since those long years of hell
Of what happened or what might have been.
We were butchers and bakers and candlestick makers
Caught up in the evils of men,
And who is to say that what happened that day
Couldn't happen all over again?

He prayed for the present, he prayed for the past,
He prayed for the things yet to be,
But for we who lay dead all the words that he said
Were as empty and hollow as he.